rain

sarinia bryant

for you;

CONTENTS

when you tell me
you don't understand
the meaning of poetry
i hear;
you don't understand
the meaning of life.

and my entire existence.

when it pours outside
there will be no umbrellas.
just me you and rain.

i could spend the entirety of a day
with no bonds or restraints.
no phones and no network.
no sound of the city.
no pressure for purpose and
no reason for reason.
i would spend more than a day
and most likely more than two.
the only things imperative
are one of me
and one of you.

you are a journey
i'm ready to embark on.
the rest was training.

some have visited,
but none moved in before you.

-my heart

i don't care whether
you're playful or petulant.
i want to bathe in your presence
and learn to love all of you.
when the sky asks
my favorite thing about you,
she will hear a symphony.
and when she asks
what i hate,
she will hear crickets.

synchronicity-

i ache when you are in pain.

as you laugh,
i heal.

i live in your laughter.
when the ground shakes and the sun falls
i will be here. still. as long as you're laughing
i'm home. but should you weep, love.
should you take your laughter away,
i would undoubtedly be lost. cold.
and possibly forgotten.

i've seen you dreaming.
i wonder where you drift to.
am i there with you?

i'm jealous of your slumber.
the way you fall heavy in it
with your breath.

my wake is a burden.

it consumes you and
i can only watch.
as your chest rises,
as it falls,
i too.

your touch is like sun.

gently it awakens me.
you're my morning light.

he whispers to me goodnight.
and i wonder if he knows
that drifting into the deep
where i cannot see nor
feel his touch. lying on that end
for the next half of morning,
will surely be the worst parts
of today and tomorrow.
goodnight,
i reply.

take off your armor.
you're a man who needs comfort.
wrap yourself in me.

i find poetry in our differences.
like the way you drink your water.
you don't shift your weight onto one hip
like i do. you stand shoulder width apart.
both feet planted. sturdy. you drink
like a river and i drink like rain.
you think i don't notice.
as if one does not notice when
indigo meets ivory. you shake me.
i swear to god you shake me.

you take me places.
only just by holding on.
just by staying here.

my heart slows as you depart.
and as you return, i accelerate.

i've seen countless sunsets and still
never do i say, i've seen a sunset before,
i do not wish to see another. even after
the seven thousandth sunset, i will still say wow.
i will still capture a photo, as if it will be my last.
i will still stop and stare. do you see the way
i love a sunset? i plan to love you the same.

blindfolded and lost.
of all the hands in the world.
still. i would find yours.

love me with conviction.

love me like a train.

all things yield to trains.
when they see you coming for me,
they ought to not stand in your way.
i want them to know you're not
making any sudden stops.
you're not turning back around.
not anytime soon.

my sanctuary-

i am but a grain of rice.
tiny in your clutch.

i am silenced by your voice.
your mouth carries words like drinking water
and;
they fall like droplets of clarity.
i stand in your rain.
i wait for you.
i beg;

cleanse me.

there he lie adrift.
tangled in my wrinkled sheets.

belonging to me.

white cotton.
i don't look past this. i don't look to the phone
or my clothes rumpled on the floor.
i don't look to the mirror. or the time. or the door.
i only see white cotton.
i think of how we came to be in it.
tangled as we are. i'm in no hurry to leave and this,
is a revolution.

anticipation-

to miss you with a smile.
what a pretty thing.

i found a picture of the sea from some years ago.
i thought; she's changed so much since then.
if i were to return to her, she would look similar
but i would be stepping into new waters.
i suppose that is why people return to people.
when they are ever changing. and not the same,
still water.

the stars are alarmed-
the way i rise and fall for you.

the sky thinks i'm the sun.

i don't need reasons to love you.
for which reason do leaves fall in autumn.
and flowers bloom in may. for which
does the moon hold our attention at night.
and the sun decides the day. i love you
because the sky is blue. i love you because
there is no other way.

you stir in your sleep.
i place my hand upon yours.
you fall softly still.

my heart does not pound in my chest
when i see you. i'm not nervous, fearful
or angry.
it slows to a constant rate when you touch me.
where it should be.
when i am out of breath i look to you.
i place your hand on my chest for air.

(still)

regardless your strength.
there's a softness to your touch
only angels bear.

when he was mad at me
he'd take a deep breath and fill his lungs
with intolerable emotions.
and the only one he ever exhaled on me was
patience.
i swear to god. i've never loved anyone
the way that he loved me.

rain

so take me with you.
even when you're not with me.
take me in your heart.

i love you from a distance
without the need for reciprocation.
i send it to you in paper planes.
i sing it to the wind.
you have never known a love
like this.
so take it darling,
take it.

the sea envies me.
the way i steal those emerald eyes.
that smile is mine.

as i spiral down in rings of happy
they tell me i should take you lightly.
i laugh at the impossibility.

how. i ask.
with no intent to listen.

when we are together i am in one place.
and when we are apart,

i am in two.

i take you knowing you were not made
with my colors. your shades of blue might mix
with my red but you will never be crimson. we
could meet in the middle. in violet perhaps.
but i won't always see me in you.
i won't expect red.
and so i place you just above the clouds.
just under the sun.

(alongside)

when my hands push back
fight against the gravity.
pull me close to you.

my wall is made of rain.
i make it stop for you.

i will be senseless.
perhaps everyone will know
how i feel for you but you. i will be
ice cold and smoldering hot and
sometimes, just lukewarm.
that's the worst.
see you'll think i don't care 'cause
you can't read my mind but she's racing.
she romanticises everything and she's
focused on forevering-
if there were ever such a word...

oh, i'm a terrible thing to love.

rain

come away with me.
i want to make more cities
feel like home with you.

i want to miss flights with you and
spend the day in an airport. i want to
get caught in the rain before
we make it there. there being-
anywhere.
i want to get a flat tire
on our drive across the state.
i want to lose my phone or id or
anything else that might set me free.
i want to reinvent all things
labeled inconveniences because
with you,
there would be no such thing.

this power you hold;
i was blind before your love.
i'm deaf when it's gone.

if you saw him
you wouldn't think he was
doing anything extraordinary.
he was draped in my bedroom's
morning light gazing
out of the window.
bewildered i asked
what he was doing.
he looked at me and replied
with the sweetest word
i'd ever heard.

'staying.'

rain

where do you wander
when you seek tranquility-

do you look to me?

i want it to be like watching rainfall
outside my bedroom window. with a book
in one hand and my tea in the other. i want
to look next to me and see the look of content
on his face. i don't want to know what time it is
and i don't want to hear a clock so much as tick.
i want to be in the moment where the most
important thing is right now.
i want everything and nothing.
whichever way it's given to me.

insecurities-

let me rid you of them all.
find safety in me.

what's mine is yours.
this house. these hands.
this heart. these eyes.

my air belongs to you.

i want to show you
just how much i adore you.

these words are useless.

i find you in puddles. in car alarms.
the bass. i find you in white noise. the letter f.
in paintings. i find you in morning dew.
the dog's bark. invitations.
i find you without looking.
without needing.
without craving.
you show up in all things.
in all forms.
in all places.
you come to me willingly.
and acceptingly,
i take you.

i will not hinder
your growth or your progression.

i will applaud you.

i think you will change, as a matter of fact
i know it.
i will be different too. time and time again
this skin will shed, and we will be reborn again.
with each moon, our love will renew.
so my love,
we will never get tired.
we will never be together
for too long, really.

when you call to me
you will find that i am here.

i have *always* been.

i am not only here
when the weather is sweet.
in thunderstorms. in fire.
in ash you will find me.

even in charred skin.

it's like this.
i think you're incredible. i don't know if incredible
quite cuts it but it works. and then i think; well
everyone else must think so too. but i can't imagine
as much as i do. but maybe they do. let's say they do.
who are they anyway. and who am i.
does any of it make a difference.
do these thoughts even matter.
why can't i stop.
why can't i sleep.

rain

'you love like it's all
you've ever known.'

oh dear. i've known
such unloving things.
i've been so unloved.

that is why i love this way.

rain

it inspires me.
missing you is not painless-

it's necessary.

i have endured hands
being pulled away. i have endured
eyes unfocused. i have endured
the direction of your step being other
than mine. i have endured the sound
of your voice distant. unsure.
if there's one thing i know,
it's that i will endure.

i lost two havens.

leafless in a battlefield.

shelter left with you.

how do they do it, i think to myself.
how does the whole world see you
and not stop what they're doing.
how do they manage their lives
without knowing you.
speaking to you.
hearing you.
feeling you.
this power
that they carry,

can i learn it.

what else would be left.
a life without you seems bland.

tastless. silent. blind.

i smell you on strangers.
i turn around to find you, knowing,
you could not be here. i smell you
on my clothes as i open up my suitcase.
two weeks have gone by.
i smell you in my coffee.
between breakfast and dessert.
the scent of you. just for a second.
well.
it can change my whole day.

you're gone come morning.
i can think of no worse pain.

i am in mourning.

we never release the pain of parting.
we carry it. the memory. the scent of it.
it clings to our skin and we count down
the days till it will happen again.
so easily we forget the joy of reuniting.
pity.

it is just a one day celebration.

you won't let me sleep.
your lack of presence haunts me.

you won't really leave.

chaos (noun)

1. the presence of me in the absence of you.

the familiar quiet sound of nothingness
filled the room and i heard myself break-
as if shattered glass hitting the floor.
i waited for someone to come and sweep me up
but the hour dragged on.
me breaking was as silent as the room ever was.
and nothingness consumed me. as i let it.

it was such a warm embrace.

alone time is loud.
with you it's but a whisper.

each way i need more.

i give you buckets of me.
i fill them from the well of my being and
it takes nothing.
there's no running out. but you,
you give me handfuls and
it makes me wonder.
is that all the gods have given you.

(dry)

you offer your hand
for a temporary warmth.

i'd rather stay cold.

if you are not sure of us.
i cannot put sureness in anything i do.

(fickle)

you saw everything fly by.
the cars and the planes. buses and trains.
when you mention them to me i nod casually.
and you'd say, didn't you see? you were
standing right next to me. and i would think of all
the things that i saw and i see. nothing fleeting.
the wood. the planters. the window sills from
which they hang. the hue of the sky.
the chip in the paint. your inconsistency.
the erratic way you stopped loving me.
i saw everything and i said

nothing.

you do not belong
and even though you push away-

i cannot release.

(holding on)

it is our initial reaction to chase what runs.
we are lions. we are here to take what's ours.
and as human beings. as lovers.
we still cannot grasp,

that what is ours does not run from us.

(letting go)

there's only one way
i'm capable of loving.

it's all or nothing.

teach me how to love in fractions.

my love is like rain.
you curse it when it comes.
it is not a warm summer's day.
not a steady flat heat.
it sprinkles and it pours and
it floods your driveway.
sometimes it's simple and
sometimes it's mad.
yes. my love is like rain.
and you curse it when it comes.

i never loved you.
i don't crave you or need you.

these lies help me heal.

loving you is an understatement.

i will write of you
when you have forgotten me.
when i am someone else
and i've run out of stories.
i'll tell the ones we never made.
i'll tell them in such a way, oh
they'll think we made it.

settling for words
when i'd rather cut distance.

this is suffering.

i envy the birds
that chirp fiercely
in the mornings.
they've so much to say
while i,
have nothing.
but melancholy thoughts
of a sleep
with no clatter.

is there any way
to better say i miss you
that will bring you back?

not to kiss you is a sin.
not to touch you feels like prison.

(i'm in hell without you)

i am either full or i'm empty.
when i'm empty i never write.
i break up with literature.
i abandon my language.
you know it when i'm barren.
you know it like you've never known
anything else.

rain

there is such a way,
you inch your way into me
while nowhere in sight.

my love is overlooked.
it's not much noticed till it's gone.
when it's gone you find yourself searching.
in eyes. in mouths. in arms. when i
am in someone else's.

i will gladly stay
if you teach me how it's done.

leaving's all i know.

a hungry heart does not stay
where it is not fed.

i want to be exceptionally small enough
to slip through the cracks. i want to be
exponentially large enough to cause those
cracks. i want to be remarkably invincible.
and
utterly invisible.
i want to be undefinably undefinable.
essentially i, i just want to be everything
i want to be. and everything you need
from me.

rain

all these languages
i tell you i need you in-

you don't speak any.

i was drifting on a current and landed
in love. now i'm starting fires and spelling
sos in stones, in hopes that someone will come
and save me. i don't know how much longer
i'll survive on this deserted island.
for no one is here with me.

does it come alive in my hands
or do i put it to rest.

(your heart)

when you kiss my tears
i forget you caused them.
you calm my heart
and i forget you harmed it.
i get amnesia when you start
loving me
again.

it was raining hard.
both outside and inside me.
you only saw the flood.

i don't have the energy. i don't have the time.

this is what the end sounds like.

my wish is to hope you'll never miss me.
to be joyous without me wherever you go.
but that is only my wish. (to hope)
for now i pray that you crave me.
like something missing in your blood.
every step of your day.

who has your heart now?

it was just seconds ago
we were in love still.

it started with small things.
songs and scents and certain phrases.
now cities remind me of you.
states and countries.
all your languages.
you made sure if
my body ever leaves you,
my mind will not follow.
my heart will not move.

i will never be
satisfied with another
knowing you exist.

love you less;
i know not how.

you rush into me like a raging river
and
i am left flooded with emotions.
long after you're gone.

long after you're gone.

heartache's a city
made for passing, not living.

never unpack there.

i didn't have the luxury of heartache.
when you walked away my whole body went numb.

as a child
i was told not to ask too many questions
unless they were intelligent.
when i was four years old i said,
i wonder what it feels like to be dead.
i was put in ,time out' in the corner of the room.
my father wasn't too harsh really, just afraid.
he didn't like the idea of me and death.
i didn't like the thought of him dead either,
but he is now. and i'm still here.
not asking too many questions.

(quiet girl)

rain

snooze the alarm, love.
there's nothing that needs you more
than my eager limbs.

i wish i could transport
to where you are.
and what's worse,
than longing to be closer
to someone so far away-
who's sleeping right
next to you.

just this once i plead.

let it be okay to need.

let me need you now.

i want you. he said.
i want you more than money and gold.
i want you like man wants to sin.
i want you in all the most selfish of ways.
i want you. but you won't let me in.
to which i replied;

need me.

i can't give you the moon.

but i can make you feel like
it's already yours.

perhaps you can't grasp
the way i love you.
and won't know it till one day
when you're sitting at the dining room
table. and the moon is beaming at you
through the window. and all the stars
will be watching you too,

but not the way that she does.

when the moon is sky's light
i know you're mine for the night.

i beg sun; *don't rise.*

you miss me when i leave.
i miss you when i know you're leaving.

minds are seasons.
(un)certainty is wind.

it passes.

what a blessing.
it's such a curse.
when i'm sure about me.
when i'm sure about you.
when i'm not.

what makes you shiver.

is my grasp not warm enough.

is my love too faint.

you left with december;
and every summer i'm convinced
i'm missing the winter's cold. i wait for it.
i hang my coat by the door.
but rain comes and it feels wrong.
i don't belong to it.
so i go back inside
and i wait for june.
assured.
it's the summer's heat
i am missing.

i'm trying to grieve.
at the same time, i'm trying,

not to resent you.

(buried)

a churning inside my chest
like forcing the hands of a clock
to go counter.
that is what it felt like
when you left.

(unnatural)

my father's leaving was his biggest teaching.

look what happens when a man leaves.
even when the most important man leaves.
look what happens.

you survive.

my eyes are rain.
my love is dry.

my dreams are of the contrary.

every time you leave, my world ends
and i have to start a new one without
you. so forgive me, for i know not
what to do with you now. my new world
shakes and quivers at the sight of you.

how many worlds must end before you stay.

i told you to leave
but i thought you knew women,
and that i meant *stay*.

i told you not to call and then i waited
by the phone.

i am teaching myself another way
or else, i'm sure i will lose you.
the way i tell you to leave with my
silence.
the way i ask you to stay with my
silence.

the more i keep you afar,
the closer i'll stay to myself
when you leave.

i'll never stick a needle
in my veins to feel something
other than life. i'll take the pain of sadness
as it comes and let the outcome ignite me.
it takes a little longer to get high from the light
at the end of the tunnel. but it's so much more
worth the waiting. life is so much more
worth living than leaving.
i'll always thank you
for that lesson, B.

the learning of love may take my whole life.
but to master the art of heartache-

just one moment.

do you see the way
in which the trees sway?
the wind is inconsistent and indefinite.
take a look at my swaying heart.
your love is that of the wind.

his love is the kind
you don't much feel
till it's gone.
when it's gone
you hear nothing
but his name.

i don't need to sleep.
dreaming of you is constant.
it starts in my wake.

they say where there's a will there's a way
but i'm losing my will and i can't find my way.
the grass is brown on both sides and i'm
drowning in the rain i should be using to water it.
i'm asleep during my wake.
i'm awake in my bed.
i should tell you i love you more.
sarinia,

i should tell you i love you more.

rain

there was no calm.
i blew in like a hurricane
all storm.
you didn't have time to prepare
no coat. no umbrella.
i poured down on you
no warning.
not a single cloud in the sky-
just me.

just rain.

when we seem finished-
when we have burned to ashes-
i will ignite us.

you're using maps and thesauruses.
dictionaries. you try to break locks
and crack codes just to figure me out.
it's tiring and it's needless.
like a foreign language or oxygen.
the birth of the world.
i am not made to be
understood sometimes.

simply appreciated.

rain

i gave you my soul
but darkness fell quick.
i'm gonna need that light back.

my mission is to create
the sweetest happiness
i can for you. to live it. to share it.
but i will still write of darkness.
to show you where i came from.
to show you what i'm made of.
so you won't be mistaken.
you won't say, look at that joyful girl.
she was born smiling. oh no.

you won't be saying that.

everything around us
may seem to be in ruins.
but repeat after me;

we. are. not. ruined.

some people were born sturdy. not us.
we were made to crumble. to rebuild.
this is how we strengthen. i'm a little
unsure about anyone who has never been
bro-ken.

this ain't a you and i thing.
it's a we thing.

-the universe

young girl.
you may have thought it was the end
when you came out of your mother's womb.
and here you live.
you may have thought it was the end
when your father left. your lover left.
your brother left. and here you live.
you may think it is the end
again with a heartbreak. again with a letdown.
again when you lose your way. again when you
hate yourself. your perimeters will change.
your body. your mind. someone's words
will mean more to you than they should but
yours will be the least kind.
i have two promises for you–
you will cry like rain.
and here you'll live.

when you are in need
there's nowhere i'd rather be
than here. beneath your heaviness.

put your weight on me.

you will come across people
too tired to love you.
let them rest.
there are people
who haven't slept in years
without you.
there are people
who only sleep to dream
about you.

to be alone and to feel alone.
those are awfully different things.
i've felt more alone with people
than i ever did
alone.

it took so long to know myself.
how long should i hope it takes you.
sunrise i wake and i say,
i'm hoping you'll get me today.
from the curve in my voice.
from the dark in my stare.
from the angst in my move.
i'm hoping you'll get me.

if you still don't realize you're holding magic-

watch me disappear.

with you i'm complete.
without you there's no difference.

i'm still the whole pie.

do you think i am lonely
because
i am without you?
i am only lonely
when i am without myself.
and you did not take any of that
with you.

even when i was mad at you,
i never stopped loving you.
how could i be so quick to
abandon myself.

i am not the girl of your dreams.
i'm the woman of your reality. i awaken you.
i snap your synapses awake. i am not a
vision. i am not about falsities, fantasies or
delusion. when i speak you ought to listen
because i am the truth the whole truth and
nothing but the truth so help me god.

shouldn't it make sense.
that i am half lover. half fighter.
i am half mother. half father.

(daughter)

i wonder what they see in a girl like me.
entirely disinterested. it makes me angry.
i think of all the girls they left because they
loved too hard. i question what the science is.
to run away from safety. to run straight into
tornadoes and fires and then i stop thinking
and i open my arms and i say
'let them burn.'

(playing with fire)

it started with a spark and ended in ashes.

our love was a volatile one.

a woman is made of fire and water.
you cannot drown her.
she cannot be burned.

sometimes there is a sea
storming inside of me. other times
a barren desert. i am not all water
or land. you must be able to swim
for miles. you must know how to live
without water.

you will know survival when you enter me.

a man can acquire
all the money in the world.
and he will never be as rich
as when i loved him.

put your money where your mouth is.

i know your heart is made of gold.
i know your hands are made of steel
and your words are laced in sterling.
i know. i know that one day,
you'll thank me for only ever
treating you as human. but right now,
you're wishing to be god
and that's a wish i know
you'll be sorry for. so i sweep this floor
beneath your feet, my king.
for when your knees are ready.

(bow down)

rain

tell me it's okay
that sometimes i am not me.

sometimes i'm no good.

if you can be there when i break-
if you can witness that and stay,
you're the one i choose to build with.
i can't live in fear of earthquakes
just 'cause you'd abandon this house.

i've loved and i've lost.
i have loved and lost myself.

well. now i just love.

it was uncomfortable yet necessary.
to claw at this skin that was no longer mine.
it didn't fit. i didn't recognize it, i needed it
off me. i looked at my hands and wept.
whose were they. i stripped myself bare
and it hurt to lay in the sun.
i cried till it rained.

(growing pains)

there's no place like you
so i don't stray very far.

there's no one like home.

i used to run away.
now i am sprinting.
dashing.
back.

home is nowhere
if i do not bring me.

let me be your eyes
when you start to lose focus.

i'll guide you back home.

let me be your moon
when all you see is darkness.

i'll light the way home.

don't let dark spaces rattle your bones.
the sun is persistent in its endeavors.

(wait)

when you ask me;
how will i get through this.
how will i find resilience to trust again.
when all i see is red. how will i find softness.
how will i resurface.
i will say;
with time.

because that is what women do.

rain

you ask me how much love you should give.

more, i tell you.

always;
more.

when we feel we are not receiving
enough love. we start giving less of it.
do you see now, our insanity.
trying to solve our problems
with a bigger one.

(destruction)

air cannot flow through closed doors.
love cannot flow through a closed heart.

open them both.

if you must cry then cry properly.
do not hold thunderstorms in your throat.
do not be ashamed to let the rain hit
loud and hard. rattle the windows.
bring down the house.

we can love someone
for simply existing. but
to stay requires reason.

loving and staying. *they are never the same.*

i love you for your passion and
yes
that includes your passion for me
and
if it fades, well.
i will still love you
but
i will not stay.

have you seen me yet.
no. i know you've been looking.

but have you, *seen* me.

you tell me i'm beautiful
and i shy away blushing
towards the ground and
why
do i do that. why do i pretend
that i do not know my face is
rare. my body's bold. my walk's
miraculous. who taught me
that it was so wrong
to agree with you.

if you want my hand
then take me like you mean it.

put some spine in it.

don't hold me with soft hands.
be them calloused and worked.
willing and able.
i don't want to slip through
silky fingers.
i need to be sure your grip is firm.

(leather)

rain

i don't waste my time.
crying when the sky is grey.
blue will come again.

saying goodbye becomes easier
when you realize you're something to lose.
feel sorry for those that let go of you.
feel terribly for those that dropped
your precious hands. they will never find
another pair like yours.
but we can pray they do,
if we're nice.

when i cannot stand
i will use these hands and knees.
i will crawl to you.

isn't it amazing, that we are able to hold hands
with another human being at such a young age.
it is the most innocent form of love. yet, so much
more powerful than sex.
it is saying;
i've got you.
i'm with you.
i'm here.

there are some secrets
i will never be able to tell you.

those are the things you love about my eyes.

(enigma)

i am the girl in the field where the weeds grow.
she wears white and she smells of lavender.
she's simple and she's somehow managed to keep
her innocence. she looks at you with doe eyes.
she waits on you for answers.

i am the woman in black with red lips
sitting on the windowsill. she has her back turned
to you but her head is slightly tilted.
she's not turning all the way around.
she doesn't dance for anyone but the things
you'll do for her are endless.

i was always this way.
somewhere stuck between leather
and lace.

i am all the stars.
i am the sun and the moon.

look at all this glow.

i peel off this skin and step out of this body.
i stop walking. i start floating. this is how it feels
when you love me.

i say to myself

this is how it feels when you love me.

rain

you probably hoped
this would be a one night stand.
but you must have smelled it
on my skin.

i'm not the kind of girl
you don't call in the morning.

don't sleep with anyone
who doesn't worship your body.
in you, one should repent.
one should meet god
when he enters you.

rain

if you came to me
expecting an endless summer-

you won't last long here.

dig past the flowers and greenery
if you want to get to know me. love me
in the soil where it's dirty and gritty and
everlasting. that's where i'll be.
long after summer is gone.

(deeper)

rain

when the deep end frightens you
will you swim away.
will you leave me
treading.

why did you think
you could hold up a ship
with a heart so shallow.
you should have already known
that i would drown you.

you will never be what they scream you are.
only what you wish for.

(be careful what you whisper)

delicate yes.
lace. feathers. wings.
endurance understated.
fragile no.
glass. shatter. break.
red tape on cardboard boxes.

my softness is not to be corrected.
my soundness is not to go unnoticed.

you will make people
uncomfortable with your presence.
stand taller. be proud.

autobiography.

my calm makes you uncomfortable.
you don't know what to do with it.
you don't know how to sit in it.
i too, have some trouble with it
but i can't escape my name.

(sarinia; serene: calm, peaceful, tranquil)

be both. a lion and a sheep.
wise enough to follow and
strong enough to lead.

(august 12, 1991)

only kittens try to prove they are lions.
i have softened my roar since birth.

i am good for you. i will nourish you.
but people pass water for wine all the time.
and i'm not changing my substance.

i cannot imagine god to be all man.
with a heart so nurturing. so forgiving.
i cannot imagine god to be all woman.
with a physical strength so unwavering.
god is masculine and feminine.
fire and water. earth and air.
stone and leaf and
feather and lead.

i have prayed to many gods
and all of them have answered.
(within)

i have been loving you all my existence.
across seas. beneath skies. over mountains.
the moment i realized i loved you
was only the moment i remembered.

(continuum)

your love is my sun.
without it i am algid stone.
all this warmth i have to give
i have because you love me.

(mine)

i am stuck in the grey.
it's the wanting you to know while
telling you little.
it's hoping you're satisfied
with the bare minimum.
(i'm hoping you're not)
i'm giving i'm giving i'm selfish.
i want to be all yours
and all mine
at the same time.

set sail in another's ship.
discover their land,
swim in their waters.
savor their foods and
take in their flowers.
but every so often,
return to yourself.

your heart may be the home to many
but it is your home first.

nothing ever thrives without love.
even the sky must give love
to the ground. in order for
flowers to grow.

you. rain.
and you rain.
and you rain.
and you rain.

this is how your garden grows.

rain

thank you;

for allowing me to rain on you.

CPSIA information can be obtained
at www.ICGtesting.com
Printed in the USA
JSHW011951130420
5046JS00015B/1586